WE PRAISE YOU, O LORD!

Patricia Fritz, O.S.F.

Paulist Press

The Publisher gratefully acknowledges the use of the following materials: Scripture quotations designated (GNB) are from the *Good News Bible,* The Bible in Today's English Version, copyright © American Bible Society, 1976. Used by permission of the publisher; Scripture texts designated (NAB) are from the *New American Bible,* copyright © 1970 by The Confraternity of Christian Doctrine, Washington, D.C. and are used by permission of the copyright owner. All rights reserved; Excerpts from *The Jerusalem Bible,* copyright © 1966 by Darton, Longman & Todd, Ltd. and Doubleday & Company, Inc., are used by permission of the publisher.

ISBN: 0-8091-2518-8

Published by Paulist Press
545 Island Road, Ramsey, N.J. 07446

Printed and bound in the
United States of America

CONTENTS

FOREWORD

"The reign of God is at hand! Reform your lives and believe in the gospel!" With this proclamation Jesus began his public life. It remained a constant theme of his preaching. He wants to reign in our hearts, in our homes and in our communities. Conversion, reform and renewal are our response to the Lord's call and his free gift of grace.

Prayer helps us to discover the call of the Lord Jesus in our life. Prayer leads us, draws us to listen, to wait. In prayer we praise God for his great goodness, we thank him for his faithful love. We fall before him in our need, we confess our sinfulness.

Jesus prayed. He showed us by his example the importance of private prayer. As Jesus prayed to be open to the Father's will, so we too pray to be open to the call to follow him and to use his gifts in the service of others. He taught us also to worship and pray together.

This collection of prayers and prayer services has been prepared to help parish councils, committees, and RENEW core groups.

No amount of meetings, planning or organization will in itself renew God's people, the Church. Renewal is the work of the Spirit. It is our hope that this prayer book will help parish groups to pray spontaneously, aloud and together each time they meet. "Where two or three are gathered in my name, there am I in their midst." (Mt. 18, 20)

Bishop Raymond A. Lucker

INTRODUCTION

Parish RENEW Core groups throughout our dioceses are being asked to pray personally and as a group. All of us in our training for RENEW, have said time and time again, that prayer is the heart of RENEW. Still the question keeps coming, "What do we do when we come together for prayer?"

We need to learn from our experience with our Parish Councils, Boards, and Committees. Most of these various groups continue to function in a business organizational mode. In most settings, prayer is relegated to a brief Our Father at the beginning and a Sign of the Cross at the end. There is little or no attempt to integrate prayer into the entirety of the meeting. In some rare situations, prayer is prepared and informs the entire meeting experience. Opportunities for these groups to experience a variety of common prayer forms are almost non-existent. Very minimal attention is given to the environment for prayer. Our experience tells us that prayer is a problem.

The "We Praise You, O Lord" prayer book is a response of the Office for Lay Ministry of the Diocese of New Ulm in Minnesota to try to remedy and not repeat this *prayer problem* with RENEW Core groups.

The book contains fifteen prepared prayer services. These services around themes provide opportunities for the groups to experience a variety of prayer forms. These include: various invitations to pray; a variety of ways to pray together with psalms; options for selecting and reflecting on Scripture and other contemporary readings; variations in shared prayer and blessings. Also included is a section on the preparation of the environment and ways to plan for prayer together. It is hoped that the 'modeling' may provide the format and ease with group prayer so that RENEW Core groups and committees will be able to plan their own prayer together.

As Bishop Lucker, of the Diocese of New Ulm, states in the Foreword, "No amount of meetings, planning, or organization will in itself renew God's people, the Church. Renewal is the work of the Spirit. It is our hope that this prayer book will help parish groups to pray spontaneously, aloud, and together each time they meet." "Where two or three are gathered in my name, there am I in their midst."

1. PREPARING THE ENVIRONMENT AND PLANNING FOR PRAYER

PREPARING THE ENVIRONMENT FOR PRAYING TOGETHER

- enthrone the Bible in a prominent place
- light a candle, symbolic of Jesus Christ risen and present within and among you
- crucifix
- lighted incense, the incense rises symbolic of our prayers rising to God, our living Father
- gathering in a circle, reminding us of the way Jesus Christ, our common Faith in Him, binds us together as one
- soft music playing in the background to quiet one's heart
- less intense, indirect light during the prayer time
- place in view of all a symbol or image related to the theme of the prayer, i.e., water, plant, statue, seeds, fruits of the earth, parish goal statement, banner, etc.
- quiet your hearts, the movement of your prayer should be in a slower, reflective pace.

FORMAT FOR PLANNING PRAYER
Introduction

Beginning the Prayer

- invitation by the leader to enter into the quiet of prayer
- usual opening verses, "God, come to our assistance"
  Response: "Lord, make haste to help us"
  Followed by the Glory be... or,
- hymn of one's choice related to the theme or,
- spontaneous by the leader or,
- section of poetry or contemporary author related to theme or,
- visual media, such as slides or filmstrip or,

- listening to a song from a record or,
- a stanza from a psalm or a small section from Scripture.

Psalms and Canticles

The Book of Psalms in the Bible contains a collection of 150 religious songs or prayers. About half of these psalms are attributed to David, some are attributed to certain temple singers, for others the authors are unknown. The psalms are hymns of praise, thanksgiving and supplication. Some of the psalms were prayers of individuals, some were of a community of people.

Select a Psalm or Several Psalms
- pray the psalm together, remembering to pray it slowly, savor each word or,
- one person prays the psalm aloud slowly and reflectively, others listen attentively or,
- each person reads a phrase or section or,
- divide the group into two sections and pray the verses alternately or,
- pray canticles.

Word of God

We often think that prayer is speaking to God, and that is true. Our speaking to God is not the most important part of prayer. The listening to God is what is of utmost and primary importance in prayer. God speaks to us in His Word. Essential to prayer together, and individually, is listening to the Word.

Select a Scripture Text
- related to the theme of the prayer or,
- from the readings of the Mass of the day or,
- favorite passages related to the theme.

After listening to the Word of God, allow some time of quiet. Take time to pray, you may want to repeat, "Speak, Lord, I am listening;" "Teach me, Lord, show me what you want me to hear;" or "Guide me, Lord, to look at my life in the light of these words."

Other Readings

The Scriptures are God's word to us. There are other words spoken through which we can hear God speaking to us.

Select

- a section from the writings of the Fathers of the Church or,

- select a section from papal or Church documents or,

- choose a section from a contemporary spiritual writer, or poet or,

- read a section from the life of a saint.

Prayer Together

After listening to God's Word turn to Him in prayer

- some moments of silent prayer in your heart or,

- spontaneous prayers from all present or expressed by the leader or,

- prepared prayers by the leader or other sources or,

- a litany of prayers with response by all, i.e., "For the harvest;" "For good health" with the response, "We thank you, Lord" or,

- prayers spoken by each person or,

- pray a common prayer together such as the Our Father or,

- the leader, or another person, may gather all the prayers together in a closing prayer.

Blessing

The blessing is a special invocation asking favor from God on persons gathered in prayer. It may be a sending forth at the very end of the gathering.

The blessing may be accompanied by some prayerful gesture, such as

- a placing of the hand on the head or on the shoulder of another or,
- a signing with the cross on the forehead of another or,
- a greeting of peace, handshake, embrace or,
- a raising of the hands above the head of another or over the entire group gathered.

2. THE LORD'S CALL

We are called to live obedient lives, that is, lives of unceasing prayer—'unceasing' not because of the many prayers we say but because of our alertness to the unceasing prayer of God's Spirit within and among us.
Henri Nouwen

THEME: The Lord's Call

Prepare: a lighted candle, open Bible, the crucifix, record, phonograph.

Invitation and Opening Prayer
Father, You always see the needs of Your people, and in compassion You empower each of us to bring Your Word where it is needed. As we once heard, and continue to hear Your invitation, "Come with Me into the fields," help us to respond joyfully and generously. May our worry never be how weary our arms grow, nor how thin our shoes become; but rather let our only concern be that we are sent as Jesus was, in the power of the Spirit to free the oppressed and to give new life.

Listen to Song
Come With Me Into the Fields (St. Louis Jesuits)

Word of God
1. Jesus continued his tour of all the towns nd villages. He taught in their synagogues, he proclaimed the good news of God's reign, and he cured every sickness and disease. At the sight of the crowds, his heart was moved with pity. They were lying prostrate from exhaustion, like sheep without a shepherd. He said to his disciples: "The harvest is good but laborers are scarce. Beg the harvest master to send out laborers to gather his harvest." (Mt. 9:35-38)

2. It was not you who chose me, it was I who chose you to go forth and bear fruit. Your fruit must endure, so that all you ask the Father in my name he will give you. (John 15:16)

Jeremiah's Call- Jeremiah 1:4-9
The word of Yahweh was addressed to me, saying

'Before I formed you in the womb I knew you;
before you came to birth I consecrated you;
I have appointed you as prophet to the nations'

I said, 'Ah, Lord Yahweh; look, I do not know how to speak: I am a child!'

7

But Yahweh replied,
'Do not say, "I am a child."
Go now to those to whom I send you
and say whatever I command you.
Do not be afraid of them,
for I am with you to protect you—
it is Yahweh who speaks!'

Then Yahweh put out his hand and touched my mouth and said to me:

'There! I am putting my words into your mouth.'

Reflection

Who were the persons who first made known to you God's call? What did you see? Hear? Who helps you respond today? Who challenges you to hear His voice today and to harden not your heart?

Sharing

Rarely does the Lord speak directly; most often He speaks through another. If anyone would like to share a name or names of people who helped them in their vocational choice, or the manner in which they were helped by people, please do so.

Psalm 21

(pray reflectively, alternating sides) from *Psalms Now* by Brandt

I. O God, in the strength and grace that You daily grant,
   we find reason for celebration.

II: You have totally fulfilled our innermost longings.
    You have responded to our deepest needs.

I: We asked for security, and You encompassed us with love,
   We looked to You for life, and You granted us life eternal.

II: We sought for identity and You adopted us as Your children,
    Whatever is of value and worth in our life has come by way of You.

I: Our hearts are glad in the realization of Your eternal presence,
   We know that we will never lose Your love.

II: We raise our voices in praise, O God,
    Because no one can separate us from You.

All: We thank You for the invitation to walk with You into the fields and we thank you for the many people who have brought us closer to You. Grant Your special blessing on those who have been a part of our call and help us to be available and responsive to others who are hearing Your call and who need someone to walk with them. Amen.

Closing Hymn   *Come With Me Into the Fields* (St. Louis Jesuits)

3. WE RESPOND TO THE LORD'S CALL AND TURN BACK TO HIM

In prayer, the Lord begins, He initiates; we receive and respond.

James V. Gau, SJ

THEME: We Respond to the Lord's Call and Turn Back to Him

Prepare: unlighted candle, dim lighting, crucifix in prominent view.

Invitation

Leader: Grace and peace be with you from God the Father and from Jesus Christ who loved us and washed away our sins in his blood.

Response: The Lord be with you.

Prayer

(take turns praying sections)

1. Almighty and merciful God, you have brought us together in the name of your Son to receive your forgiveness, your love and your strength.

2. Open our eyes to see the evil we have done, renew us in spirit to be servants of your truth.

3. Reconcile by your love those divided by sin. Heal and strengthen by your power those wounded by human weakness.

4. Raise up by your spirit those who have lost the life of grace.

5. Give us new heart to love you, so that our lives may reflect the image of your Son.

   All: May the world see the glory of Christ revealed in your Church, and come to know that he is the one whom you have sent, Jesus Christ, your Son our Lord for ever and ever.

   Amen.

Word of God

Galatians 5:16-25

Let me put it like this: if you are guided by the Spirit you will be in no danger of yielding to self-indulgence. • Since self-indulgence is the opposite of Spirit, the Spirit is totally against such a thing, and it is precisely because the two are so opposed that you do not always carry out your good intentions. • If you are led by the Spirit, no law can touch you. • When self-indulgence is at work the results are obvious: fornication, gross indecency and sexual irresponsibility; idolatry and sorcery; feuds and wrangling, jealousy, bad temper and quarrels; disagreements, factions, envy; drunkenness, orgies and similar things. • I warn you now, as I warned you before: those who behave like this will not inherit the kingdom of God. • What the Spirit brings is very different: love, joy, peace, patience, kindness, goodness, trustfulness, • gentleness and self-control. There can be no law against things like that, of course. • You cannot belong to Christ Jesus unless you crucify all self-indulgent passions and desires.

Since the Spirit is our life, let us be directed by the Spirit.

Reflection

The law of love is the first commandment. The Spirit attracts us to the good, frees us from mere slavish following of the law, helps us to see the value expressed by the law.

Sin is selfishness as found within our human relationships...a disrupting of community life in love.

Litany for Forgiveness

Leader: In peace, let us pray to the Lord:
For the healing of all our sins, let us...

Response: Lord have mercy.

Leader: We have dishonored his name by using it in anger and carelessness, for his healing, let us...

Response: Lord have mercy.

Leader: We have not trusted in God and despaired of his love and mercy, for his healing, let us...

Response: Lord have mercy.

Leader: We have not shown our love, and our thanks to him by worshipping him faithfully, for his healing, let us...

Response: Lord have mercy.

Leader: We have sinned against our brothers and sisters, for their forgiveness and his healing, let us...

Response: Lord have mercy.

Leader: We have been thoughtless and careless toward the needs of our neighbors, especially those who are closest to us, for his healing, let us...

Response: Lord have mercy.

Leader: We have led others to evil thoughts or deeds, for his healing, let us...

Response: Lord have mercy.

Leader: We have been uncommitted to spread peace, joy, and justice, especially among the poor and those who suffer because of prejudice, bigotry, and war, for his healing, let us...

Response: Lord have mercy.

Leader: We have all failed to feed Christ in the hungry, clothe him in the naked, visit him in prison and the sickroom, for his healing, let us...

Response: Lord have mercy.

Leader: We have complained against authority and law because they seem to block our selfish ends and have not seen in them a way to the common good, for his healing, let us...

Response: Lord have mercy.

Leader: We have indeed sinned against the Lord in our self-development, for his healing, let us...

Response: Lord have mercy.

Leader: We have failed to fulfill ourselves in our vocations, for his healing, let us...

Response: Lord have mercy.

Leader: We have been guilty of harmful excesses of many kinds, for his healing, let us...

Response: Lord have mercy.

Leader: We have blindly and comfortably conformed to the crowd to avoid the task of personal growth unto maturity, for his healing, let us...

Response: Lord have mercy.

Let us pray together the Confiteor:

I confess to almighty God, and to you my brothers and sisters, that I have sinned through my own fault, in my thoughts and in my words, in what I have done and in what I have failed to do; and I ask Blessed Mary, ever virgin, all the angels and saints, and you, my brothers and sisters, to pray for me to the Lord our God.

Sign of Peace   (sign a cross on the forehead of one another with the words—) "May you be healed from sin and turn toward God and know His peace."

Then all gather in a circle and then light the candle as the leader says:

Leader: "As I light this candle, let it be a reminder to each of us that

Jesus is our way, our truth and our light—may we respond to His call each day and turn to Him with all our hearts."

Response: Amen.

Blessing

(leader raises a hand over the group)

Leader: Go and proclaim to all the wonderful works of God.

Response: Amen.

Leader: Go and tell all about the God who has brought you salvation.

Response: Amen.

4. EMPOWERMENT BY THE SPIRIT

In prayer, the Spirit calls us to penetrate the bounds of our consciousness to see not ourselves but God as the center of the universe.

James V. Gau, SJ

THEME: Empowerment by the Spirit

Prepare: lighted candle; open Bible; pictures of the poor, hungry, war-torn people; banner of the Holy Spirit.

Invitation   **Leader:** Come Holy Spirit, open our eyes to Your presence in our lives.

All: We adore you Who dwell in our hearts. Give us the grace to honestly face what our response to Your presence in our lives has been in the past. Give us an understanding heart that we may hear Your voice—through Your Word, Your inspirations, and through Your people. Give us Your vibrant Spirit to enable us to go forth today empowered to love tenderly, to act justly, and to walk humbly with our God.   Amen.

Psalm 25:4-11   (alternate sides)

I: Yahweh, make your ways known to me, teach me your paths.

II: Set me in the way of your truth, and teach me, for you are the God who serves me.

I: All day long I hope in you because of your goodness, Yahweh.

II: Remember your kindness, Yahweh, your love that you showed long ago.

I: Do not remember the sins of my youth; but rather, with your love, remember me.

II: Yahweh is so good, so upright, he teaches the way to sinners;

I: In all that is right, he guides the humble, and instructs the poor in his ways.

II: All Yahweh's paths are love and truth for those who keep his covenant and his decrees.

I: For the sake of your name, Yahweh, forgive my guilt, for it is great.

All: Glory be...

Word of God   Matthew 25:31-46 (NAB)

"When the Son of Man comes in his glory, escorted by all the angels of heaven, he will sit upon his royal throne, and all the nations will be assembled before him. Then he will separate them into two groups, as a shepherd separates sheep from goats. The sheep he will place on his right hand, the goats on his left. The king will say to those on his right: 'Come. You have my Father's blessing! Inherit the kingdom prepared for you from the creation of the world. For I was hungry and you gave me food, I was thirsty and you gave me drink. I was a stranger and you welcomed me, naked and you clothed me. I was ill and you comforted me, in prison and you came to visit me.' Then the just will ask him: 'Lord when did we see you hungry and feed you or see you thirsty and give you drink? When did we welcome you away from home or clothe you in your nakedness? When did we visit you when you were ill or in prison?' The king will answer them: 'I assure you, as often as you did it for one of my least brothers, you did it for me.'

"Then he will say to those on his left: 'Out of my sight, you condemned, into that everlasting fire prepared for the devil and his angels! I was hungry and you gave me no food. I was thirsty and you gave me no drink. I was away from home and you gave me no welcome, naked and you gave me no clothing. I was ill and in prison and you did not come to comfort me.' Then they in turn will ask: 'Lord, when did we see you hungry or thirsty or away from home or naked or ill or in prison and not attend you in your needs?' He will answer them: 'I assure you, as often as you neglected to do it to one of these least ones, you neglected to do it to me.' These will go off to eternal punishment and the just to eternal life."

Reflection Lord, have I been guilty? Help me to see where and when.

"Have I been insensible to the needs of the poor, or let a widow's eyes grow dim?

Or taken my share of bread alone, not giving a share to the orphan?

Have I ever seen someone in need of clothing, or a beggar going naked, without his having cause to bless me from his heart—as he felt the warmth of the fleece from my lambs?

Have I put all my trust in gold, from finest gold sought in my security?

Have I gloated over my great wealth, or the riches that my hands have won?

Have I taken pleasure in my enemies' misfortunes, or made merry when disaster overtook them?

The people of my tent, did they not say, 'Is there a man he has not filled with meat?'

No stranger ever had to sleep outside, my door was always open to the traveler."

Leader: Do not be afraid! For Jesus tells us, "I am always with you and I have sent my Spirit to teach you all things!"

Shared Prayer Share your individual prayers for forgiveness and strength to act for justice.

Closing Prayer (together)

Almighty and eternal God,
    may your grace enkindle in all persons
    a love for the many unfortunate people

whom poverty and misery reduce
   to a condition of life
   unworthy of human beings.
Arouse in the hearts of those
   who call you Father
a hunger and thirst for social justice
   and for fraternal charity in deeds
   and in truth.
Grant, O Lord, peace in our days,
   peace to souls,
   peace to our country
   and peace among nations.

      Amen.

               —Pope Pius XII

Blessing   (the leader raises his right hand over the group)

Leader: "The Spirit of the Lord is upon you."
Response: Amen.

Leader: "He has anointed you to preach the Good News to the poor."
Response: Amen.

Leader: "He has sent you to proclaim liberty to captives."
Response: Amen.

Leader: "And the recovery of sight to the blind, to set free the oppressed."

Response: Amen.

Leader: "And may Almighty God, Father, Son and Spirit strengthen us in the mission of justice and peace."

Response: Amen.

5. DISCIPLESHIP: WHAT IS THE COST TO ME?

To pray means to open hands before God. It means slowly relaxing the tension which squeezed your hands together and accepting your existence with an increasing readiness, not as a possession to defend but as a gift to receive.

Henri Nouwen

THEME: Discipleship: What Is the Cost to Me?

Prepare: lighted candle; symbols of service; open Bible.

Invitation

Leader: What does it mean to take Jesus seriously?

Response: To be open to the Father, Creator of life; to Jesus, the Lord of my life; to the Spirit, the Life of my life.

Leader: What is the cost of discipleship?

Response: It is to empty myself out, to go, to open myself to suffering in my life, to have the mind of Christ Jesus.

Psalms 133 and 134

(alternating sides) *Psalms Now* by Brandt

I: O God, how precious it is for us
And how pleasing it must be to You
When your sons and daughters learn how to live
and work together in unity!

II: It is in the measure that we do this that we
begin to resemble You
And to carry out most effectively your purposes
In our disjointed and discordant world.

I: Come, let us together bless His name,
Rejoice in His loving concern for us,
Declare his worth to all creatures,
And walk in obedience to His call.

II: It is the same God who made heaven and earth
And all of us who dwell therein.
Let us worship and serve Him together.

Closing Prayer   (persons read section) 1 John 4:7-12

1. My dear people,
   let us love one another
   since love comes from God
   and everyone who loves is begotten by God and knows God.

2. Anyone who fails to love can never have known God,
   because God is love.
   God's love for us was revealed
   when God sent into the world his only Son
   so that we could have life through him;

3. this is the love I mean:
   not our love for God,
   but God's love for us when he sent his Son
   to be the sacrifice that takes our sins away.

4. My dear people,
   since God has loved us so much,
   we too should love one another.

   All: No one has ever seen God;
   but as long as we love one another
   God will live in us
   and his love will be complete in us.

Closing Hymn   *Sent Forth by God's Blessing* Verse 2

With praise and thanksgiving to God who is living,
The tasks of our ev'ry-day life we embrace.
Our faith ever sharing, in love ever caring,

We claim as our own all people as one.
One bread that has fed us, one light that has led us
Unite us as one in his life that we share.
Then may all the living with praise and thanksgiving
Give honor to Christ and his name that we bear.

Word of God   Ephesians 1:3-12

Blessed be God the Father of our Lord Jesus Christ,
who has blessed us with all the spiritual blessings of heaven in Christ.
Before the world was made, he chose us, chose us in Christ,
to be holy and spotless, and to live through love in his presence,
determining that we should become his adopted sons, through Jesus
    Christ
for his own kind purposes,
to make us praise the glory of his grace,
his free gift to us in the Beloved,
in whom, through his blood, we gain our freedom, the forgiveness of
    our sins.
Such is the richness of the grace
which he has showered on us
in all wisdom and insight.
He has let us know the mystery of his purpose,
the hidden plan he so kindly made in Christ from the beginning
to act upon when the times had run their course to the end:
that he would bring everything together under Christ, as head,
everything in the heavens and everything on earth.
And it is in him that we were claimed as God's own,
chosen from the beginning,
under the predetermined plan of the one who guides all things

as he decides by his own will;
chosen to be,
for his greater glory,
the people who would put their hopes in Christ before he came.

**Reflection
and Sharing**

1. Who is Jesus for me?

2. What kinds of personal decisions have I made to be a Christian?

3. How has my own life experience called me to a deeper awareness of being a Christian?

4. What kind of social witness do I give as a Christian in, for example, world hunger, poverty, war, nuclear weapons, discrimination, others?

5. What do I think is the cost of discipleship?

**Prayer of Praise
and
Thanksgiving**

Leader: Father, you have given us so much to be thankful for throughout our lives. You have even revealed yourself to us as a community and given us a command to do what is most life-giving—love one another in community. We wish to place before you now our prayers of gratitude for these and for your other blessings on us.

Leader: For calling us together as adults in Christian Community in the Church of (name of your church)...

Response: We thank you, Lord.

Leader: For the freedom to grow in life and vision, individuality, and vibrant hope...

Response: We thank you, Lord.

Leader: For the ever-abiding presence of your Holy Spirit, who binds us in meaningful love...

Response: We thank you, Lord.

Leader: For the affection and encouragement, sympathy, truth and love of those in our communities...

Response: We thank you, Lord.

Leader: Individual petitions...

Response: We thank you, Lord.

6. EVANGELIZATION: WE PROCLAIM THE GOSPEL SO THAT FAITH MAY BE AROUSED, UNFOLDED AND GROW

"...for when we cannot choose words in order to pray properly, the Spirit...expresses our plea in a way that could never be put into words, and God who knows everything in our hearts knows perfectly well what He means..."

Romans 8:26-27
Jerusalem Bible

THEME: We Proclaim the Gospel So That Faith May Be Aroused, Unfolded and Grow

Prepare: lighted candle, open Bible, record, phonograph.

Invitation

We gather together to cultivate the Word of God in the hearts of all. In our Evangelization, we will meet people whose ears are foreign to the Words of God. Some who have not yet heard or understood, "Jesus"— the seed of God's love. There are others who understand God's Love, and wish now to come closer to Him.

This is our mission—to encourage all to realize the presence of God in their hearts. Let us always remember that..."Some will till, some will sow, and some will harvest," yet all people shine in the radiance of God's love.

Hymn

Build the City of God (St. Louis Jesuits)

Prayer

God our Father,
You sent Your Son into the world to be its true light.
Pour out the Spirit he promised us
to sow the truth in the hearts of all people
and awaken in them obedience to the faith.
May all be born again to new life in baptism
and enter the fellowship of your one holy people.

Grant this through our Lord Jesus Christ, your Son,
who lives and reigns with you and the Holy Spirit,
one God, for ever and ever. Amen.

Word of God

1 Cor. 3:1-9

As a matter of fact, my brothers (and sisters), I could not talk to you as I talk to people who have the Spirit; I had to talk to you as though you belonged to this world, as children in the Christian faith. I had to feed you milk, not solid food, because you were not ready for it. And even now you are not ready for it, because you still live as the people of this world live. When there is jealousy among you and you quarrel with one another, doesn't this prove that you belong to this world, living by its standards? When one of you says, "I follow Paul," and another, "I follow Apollos"—aren't you acting like worldly people?

After all, who is Apollos? And who is Paul? We are simply God's servants, by whom you were led to believe. Each one of us does the work which the Lord gave him to do: I planted the seed, Apollos watered the plant, but it was God who made the plant grow. The one who plants and the one who waters really do not matter. It is God who matters, because he makes the plant grow. There is no difference between the one who plants and the one who waters; God will reward each one according to the work done. For we are partners working together for God, and you are God's Field.

This is the Word of the Lord.

Response: Thanks be to God.

Luke 10:1-2 (GNB)

After this the Lord chose another seventy-two men and sent them out two by two, to go ahead of him to every town and place where he himself was about to go. He said to them, "There is a large harvest, but few workers to gather it in. Pray to the owner of the harvest that he will send out workers to gather in his harvest."

This is the Gospel of the Lord.

Response: Praise to you, Lord Jesus Christ.

**Church
Documents**

*The Evangelization of the Modern World,
Synod of Bishops, 1973. Sections 3, 4.*

This salvific presence of Christ is realized through the medium of the
Church: God wills all men to be saved in the unity of the People of God
and through the ministry of this People. The Church's mediation is
accomplished through evangelization.

The word "evangelization" is commonly understood in several different
senses today. In the first place, the term can mean every activity
whereby the world is in any way transformed in accordance with the will
of God the Creator and Redeemer. Secondly, the word is used to mean
the priestly, prophetic and royal activity whereby the Church is built up
according to Christ's intention. A third and more common meaning is
the activity whereby the Gospel is awakened in non-Christians and
fostered in Christians (missionary preaching, catechetics, homiletics,
etc.).

Finally, the word, "evangelization" is restricted to meaning the first
proclamation of the Gospel to non-Christians, whereby faith is
awakened.

Outside Spiritual Reading:

- *The Evangelization of the Modern World, Synod of Bishops, 1973*
  Available from:
    Publications Office
    USCC
    1312 Massachusetts Ave., N.W.
    Washington, D.C. 20005

**Reflection
and Sharing**

1. How can we make our parish community aware that they are respon-
   sible for the evangelization both of their own members and of those
   who either do not believe or who have lost the faith?

2. How can our parishes become real communities? How can they work together to foster community life?

3. How can we ensure that the Church is present in the "world of work"?

4. Does the Church, your parish community, show that she shares Christ's special love for the poor?

Closing Prayer Father, in Your invitation is our peace,
and in Your call, is our hope.
Be present to all those who need to know that they belong.
Help us to represent each person's experience of You,
and the paths that they take to find You.
If we lose our way, Father,
bring us home and welcome us once more.
Amen.

7. OUR MISSION— WE ARE SENT

"Offer yourselves as a living sacrifice to God, dedicated to His service and pleasing to Him. This is the true worship that you should offer. Do not conform yourselves to the standards of this world, but let God transform you inwardly by a complete change of your mind. Then, you will be able to know the will of God—what is good and is pleasing to Him and is perfect."

Romans 12:1-2
Good News Bible

THEME: Our Mission—We Are Sent

Prepare: lighted candle, open Bible, Mission Statement of the community or Diocese (copy for each).

Invitation

Leader: Let us begin our prayer, "In the name of the Father, and of the Son and of the Holy Spirit"

Response: Amen.

Leader: The word "Mission" means "to be sent." As Jesus said, "As the Father sent me, so I also send you." Jesus had a mission, the Church universal has a mission. We as the Church are sent on a mission.

Response: You called us to this mission, strengthen us to carry it out.

Leader: We form one people,—Bishop, priests, religious, and laity. We are bound together as a communion (community) of one faith, one divine life, one call to love, celebrating the same sacraments with Jesus as our center and the Holy Spirit as our source of life and power.

Response: You called us to this mission, strengthen us to carry it out.

Leader: No matter how you put it, the mission of the Church must be the same as the mission of Jesus.

Response: You called us to this mission, strengthen us to carry it out.

Psalm 119:1-2,
4-5, 17-18,
33-34

(alternate sides) (NAB)

I: Happy are they whose way is blameless,
    who walk in the law of the LORD.
Happy are they who observe his decrees,
    who seek him with all their heart.

II: You have commanded that your precepts
      be diligently kept.
   Oh, that I might be firm in the ways of
      keeping your statutes!

 I: Be good to your servant, that I may live
      and keep your words.
   Open my eyes, that I may consider the
      wonders of your law.

II: Instruct me, O LORD, in the way of your statutes,
      that I may exactly observe them.
   Give me discernment, that I may observe your law,
      and keep it with all my heart.

   All: Glory be...

Word of God   John 15:4, 5, 16

Make your home in me, as I make mine in you.
As a branch cannot bear fruit all by itself,
but must remain part of the vine,
neither can you unless you remain in me.

I am the vine,
you are the branches,
Whoever remains in me, with me in him,
bears fruit in plenty;
for cut off from me you can do nothing.

You did not choose me,
no, I chose you;
and I commissioned you
to go out and to bear fruit,
fruit that will last;
and then the Father will give you
anything you ask him in my name.

Reflection

Leader: We have been called. We have been chosen. We have been sent. We wish to consider what that call means in our lives. Where have we been sent? Where am I being sent now? Have I taken risks in the past? Am I willing to be sent by the Holy Spirit to take risks in the future? Have I felt the Lord with me? Let us consider the example of those who have been sent before us. (each take a section—pause after each)

1. Make us strong with the faith of our father Abraham.

2. Make us bold with the courage of Moses, the leader of Your chosen people.

3. Enlighten us with the wisdom of Samuel, ruler and judge of Israel.

4. Give us the Spirit of discernment and decision so that we may work in Your service with the authority of the great King David.

5. Make us alive as You did the prophet Isaiah, with a sense of Your holy presence.

6. Give us, as You gave John the Baptist, a love for poverty and self-effacement in our labors for the spread of Your Kingdom.

7. Make us great-hearted, like Paul, so that we may be all things to all people in Christ Jesus.

8. Shape us, transform us, even as You made the Virgin Mary, the perfect instrument in Your hands.

9. With Jesus, our Brother, we hear the call, with Him we answer:

   All: Father, Your will be done in us.

Prayer

Leader: Let us stand to pray for the grace to receive God's Spirit. You are the People of God. He has loved you and chosen you for His own.

Response: Anoint me with Your Spirit; send me to proclaim Good News.

Leader: You have been chosen in Christ to be the Father's adopted children.

Response: Anoint me with Your Spirit; send me to proclaim Good News.

Leader: Come together, love one another the way that He has first loved you.

Response: Anoint me with Your Spirit; send me to proclaim Good News.

Leader: You have been sent to proclaim Good News to the poor, release to those held bound, and fullness of joy to the broken-hearted.

Response: Anoint me with Your Spirit; send me to proclaim Good News.

Leader: Your mission is to be renewed by His love and strengthened by His grace.

Response: Anoint me with Your Spirit; send me to proclaim Good News.

Leader: You shall be prophet to the nations, a teacher to all people.

Response: Anoint me with Your Spirit; send me to proclaim Good News.

Leader: Go now to the whole world. You are sent as His messenger, empowered by His Spirit, enlivened by His Word.

Response: Anoint me with Your Spirit; send me to proclaim Good News.

Leader: Let us pray together, in the words that Jesus taught us, Our Father...

Blessing

Leader: May God our Father complete the work He has begun and keep the gifts of His Spirit active in your hearts.

Response: Amen.

Leader: May you be ready to live His Gospel, eager to do His will, and enthusiastic in proclaiming His Word.

Response: Amen.

Leader: May you never be ashamed to proclaim to all the world Christ crucified and risen.

Response: Amen.

Closing Hymn   *Be Not Afraid* (St. Louis Jesuits)

8. WE ARE THE CHURCH— "YOU, TOO, ARE LIVING STONES"

A prayer makes sense only if it is 'lived', unless life and prayer become completely interwoven, prayers become a sort of polite madrigal which you offer to God at moments when you are giving time to Him.

Anthony Bloom

THEME: We Are the Church—"You, Too, Are Living Stones"

Invitation   To be a member of the Church is to belong to a special group—a holy people. It is to be called and formed by God to serve Him and our brothers and sisters.

(pause)

All: Lord, we come into your presence.
With praise and thanksgiving.
Glory be...

Psalm 149   (each person pray a section) paraphrase

1. Sing a new song to the Lord,
   His praise in the assembly of the faithful.

2. Let Israel rejoice in its maker,
   let Zion's people exult in their king.

3. Let them praise His name with dancing
   and make music with timbrel and harp.

4. For the Lord takes delight in his people.
   He crowns the poor with salvation.

5. Let the faithful rejoice in their glory,
   shout for joy and take their rest.
   Let the praise of God be on their lips.

All: Glory be...

(pause)

Psalm 115   (alternate sides) paraphrase

   I: Not to us, is the honor due, God
     Not to us, but to you alone.
     For you are reliable mercy and love.
     God here among us.

  II: How, then, can there be people who ask:
     "Where is that God of yours?"
     Our God is above everything,
     what he wants he makes.

   I: People of God, always keep trusting,
     He is your help and your shield.

  II: The Lord God keeps us in his heart
     and gives us his blessing.

   All: Glory be...

   (pause)

Word of God   1 Peter 2:4-5, 9-10

He is the living stone, rejected by men but chosen by God and precious to him; set yourselves close to him • so that you too, the holy priesthood that offers the spiritual sacrifices which Jesus Christ has made acceptable to God, may be living stones making a spiritual house.

But you are a *chosen race, a royal priesthood, a consecrated nation, a people set apart* to sing the praises of God who called you out of the darkness into his wonderful light. • Once you were *not a people* at all and now you are the People of God; once you were *outside the mercy* and now *you have been given mercy.*

This is the Word of the Lord.

All: Thanks be to God.

(pause for silent reflection)

Sharing   (after some quiet time, invite all to share)

1. Why did God fashion Himself a people in the Old and the New Testament?

2. How visible is your parish as a people of God?

3. Personally, how do you feel God has chosen and fashioned you?

Prayer   Let us pray that we will be open to God, as he fashions a path for our growth to Him.

(pause for silent reflection)

God, our Father,
In your care and wisdom
You have chosen us to be your own people.
May our parish be a sign of your holiness,
may it reveal for us the presence of your love,
and may that love always grow in our lives.
Grant this through our Lord Jesus Christ, your Son,
who lives and reigns with you and the Holy Spirit,
one God, for ever and ever.

Response: Amen.

Blessing   (the leader extends his right hand over the group and extends the blessing)

Leader: "You are living stones"
Response: Amen.

Leader: "You are precious in God's Eyes"
Response: Amen.

Leader: "You are a people God claims for His Own.
Response: Amen.

9. THERE ARE DIFFERENT GIFTS, BUT THE SAME SPIRIT

In prayer, as in our lives, the Spirit speaks first, and we receive and respond.

James V. Gau, SJ

THEME: There Are Different Gifts, But the Same Spirit

Prepare: lighted candle, open Bible, record of soft instrumental music, phonograph.

Invitation

Leader: The Spirit enriches our lives by giving us His gifts and then calls them forth for the benefit of the whole community. Each day the Spirit helps us to live like new creations. Filled with the gift of His love we are enabled to take off the old self and put on the new. As we respond to His gifts we begin to recognize that we must use them in the service of others.

Response: Send out your Spirit and renew us, O Lord.

Canticle of Praise

Ephesians 1:3-10; 13-14 (alternate sides)

I: Blessed be God, the Father of our Lord Jesus Christ,
who has blessed us with the spiritual blessings of heaven
in Christ.

II: Before the world was made, he chose us, chose us in Christ
to be holy and spotless, and to live through love in his presence,

I: determining that we should become his adopted sons
(children), through Jesus Christ,
for his own kind purposes

II: to make us praise the glory of his grace,
his free gift to us in the Beloved,
in whom, through his blood, we gain our freedom, the
forgiveness of our sins.

I: Such is the richness of the grace,
which he has showered on us
in all wisdom and insight.

II: He has let us know the mystery of his purpose,
the hidden plan he so kindly made in Christ from the
beginning to act upon when the times had run their course
to the end...

I: Now you, too, in him
have heard the message of the truth and the good news of
your salvation, and have believed it;

II: and you, too, have been stamped with the seal of the Holy Spirit
and the Promise of the pledge of our inheritance
which brings freedom for those whom God has taken for his
own to make his glory praised.

All: Glory be...

Word of God   Romans 12:4-13

• Just as each of our bodies has several parts and each part has a separate
function, • so all of us, in union with Christ, form one body, and as parts

of it we belong to each other. • Our gifts differ according to the grace given us. If your gift is prophecy, then use it as your faith suggests; • if administration, then use it for administration; if teaching, then use it for teaching. • Let the preachers deliver sermons, the almsgivers give freely, the officials be diligent, and those who do works of mercy do them cheerfully.

Do not let your love be a pretence, but sincerely prefer good to evil. • Love each other as much as brothers should, and have a profound respect for each other. • Work for the Lord with untiring effort and with great earnestness of spirit. • If you have hope, this will make you cheerful. Do not give up if trials come; and keep on praying. • If any of the saints are in need you must share with them; and you should make hospitality your special care.

The Reflective Thanksgiving

Leader: Lord, God we are weak and poor. Often we are not as we want to be. We come before You in our poverty, aware that all we have and all we are and all we need is a gift from You. We have been aware of Your caring support throughout our lives. As we come before You now to reflect upon Your goodness to us, we do so with grateful hearts.

Reader 1: For the gifts of air and water and food, the light of the sun and the cool summer breezes, for all Your gifts which sustain our physical needs, we say:

All: Thank You, Lord.

Reader 2: For telling us You want to take away our fears and insecurities, we say:

All: Thank You Lord.

Reader 3: For the gifts of each other and of belonging to our family and community, we say:

All: Thank You Lord.

Reader 1: For your gift of love which enables us to love ourselves and others as You love us, we say:

All: Thank You Lord.

Reader 2: For gifts of intelligence, memory and will, and allowing us to exercise these gifts, we say:

All: Thank You, Lord.

Reader 3: For the wonderful feelings of being alive, playful, and for simplicity, order, goodness, beauty, truth, justice and peace, we say:

All: Thank You, Lord.

Leader: Let us pray together,
Lord, we thank You for all Your gifts. We realize that as You gift us, You do so to free us to love others and to love You more deeply. We ask You now to quicken our response to heal broken relationships and to see others as You see them. Help us not to center on ourselves, but upon You and Your power working within us. We ask this through Christ our Lord.

All: Amen.

Blessing

(leader extends hands over the group)

Leader: May almighty God empower you with the Spirit through the outpouring of His gifts.

Response: Amen.

Leader: May He enlighten your minds to understand His Word.

Response: Amen.

Leader: May He direct your steps so you may work to bring about His kingdom.

Response: Amen.

Leader: May almighty God bless you: Father, Son, and the Holy Spirit.

Response: Amen.

10. THE LIGHT OF FAITH

Prayer is a way of life which allows you to find a stillness in the midst of the world where you open your hands to God's promises, and find hope for yourself, your friends and the whole community in which you live.

Henri Nouwen

THEME: The Light of Faith

Prepare: lighted candle, open Bible, incense.

Invitation

Leader: We gather in prayer, with the sign of our salvation.
In the name of God, and of God's Word, and of God's Spirit.

Response: Amen.

Leader: May the grace of the Word made flesh be with you always.

Response: And also with you.

Prayer

You are a God whose Word is powerful,
is life-giving for all those who hear.
Touch with your Spirit our minds and hearts,
as we consider your Word.
Help us to find the message of your saving love.
May your Word cleanse us and awaken our trust in you,
challenge us and measure us, and help us
to judge our ways.
through Christ our Lord.

Response: Amen.

Psalm 24

(alternating sides) (GNB)

I: The world and all that is in it belong
to the Lord;
the earth and all who live on it are his.
He built it on the deep waters
beneath the earth and
laid its foundations in
the ocean depths.

II: Who has the right to go up to the Lord's hill?
   Who is allowed to enter his holy temple?
He who is pure in act and in thought,
   who does not worship idols,
      or make false promises.

I: The Lord will bless them:
   God his Savior will declare them innocent.
Such are the people who come to God,
   who come into the presence
      of the God of Jacob.

II: Fling wide the gates,
   open wide the ancient doors,
      and the great king will come in.
         Who is this great king?

I: He is the LORD, strong and mighty,
   the LORD, victorious in battle!

II: Fling wide the gates,
   open the ancient doors,
      and the great king will come in.
         Who is this great king?

I: The triumphant LORD, he is the great king!

**Church
Document**

To Teach As Jesus Did

The teaching Church calls upon each of us to have an active faith in God
and his revealed truth. Under the influence of the Holy Spirit, man gives
total adherence to God revealing Himself. Faith involves intellectual

acceptance but also much more. Through faith men and women have a new vision of God, the world, and themselves. They must not only accept the Christian message but act on it, witnessing as individuals and a community to all that Jesus said and did. Catechesis thus "gives clarity and vigor to faith, nourishes a life lived according to the spirit of Christ, leads to a knowing and active participation in the liturgical mystery, and inspires apostolic action."

In sum, doctrine is not merely a matter for the intellect, but is the basis for a way of life as envisioned by St. Paul: "Let us profess the truth in love and grow to the full maturity of Christ the head." (Ephesians, 4:15)

Faith Response   (in sections by individual readers—during this reading have incense burning and as it rises, lift up yourselves committed to the Word)

1. You yourselves are our letter of recommendation,
       written on your hearts,
          to be known and read by all;

2. and you show that you are a letter from Christ
       delivered by us,
          written not with ink
             but with the Spirit of the living God,
                not on tablets of stone
                   but on tablets of human hearts.

3. Such is the confidence that we have
       through Christ toward God.
          Not that we are sufficient of ourselves
             to claim anything as coming from us;
                our sufficiency is from God
                   who has qualified us

53

to be ministers of a new covenant,
not in a written code
but in the spirit;
for the written codes kills,
but the Spirit gives life...

1. Since we have such a hope,
we are very bold,
not like Moses,
who put a veil over his face so that
the Israelites might not see
the end of the fading splendor...

2. And we all, with unveiled face,
beholding the glory of the Lord,
are being changed into his likeness
from one degree of glory to another;
for this comes from the Lord
who is the Spirit.

3. Therefore, having this ministry
by the mercy of God,
we do not lose heart.

1. And even if our gospel is veiled,
it is veiled only
to those who are perishing.
In their case, the god of this world
has blinded the minds of the unbelievers,
to keep them from seeing the light
of the gospel of the glory of Christ
who is the likeness of God.

2. For what we preach is not ourselves,
but Jesus Christ as Lord,

with ourselves as your servants
for Jesus' sake.

3. For it is the God who said,
   'Let the light shine out of darkness,'
   who has shone in our hearts
   to give the light of the knowledge
   of the glory of God
   in the face of Christ.

Paraphrase of 2 Cor. 3:2-13; 4:1-6

Prayer

Let us pray together the prayer that Jesus taught us to pray:

All: Our Father...

Blessing

Leader: I charge you to preach the word,
   to stay with this task
      whether convenient or inconvenient...
         correcting, reproving, appealing...
            constantly preaching
               and never losing patience...
Be steady and self-possessed;
   put up with hardship,
      perform your work as an evangelist,
         fulfill your ministry.

Response: Amen.

11. ALL GLORY, PRAISE AND HONOR TO YOU, LORD GOD

Prayer is letting God draw us into intimacy with Him.

James V. Gau, SJ

THEME: All Glory, Praise and Honor to You, Lord God

Prepare: lighted candle, open Bible, a green plant—(symbol of life and hope)

Invitation

(from the *Constitution on the Sacred Liturgy*)

Leader: "...the liturgy, is the summit towards which the activity of the Church is directed: at the same time it is the fount from which all her power flows. For the aim and object of apostolic faith and baptism should come together to praise God in the midst of his Church, to take part in the sacrifice, and to eat the Lord's supper."

Response: Lord, we come into your presence with praise and thanksgiving.

Glory be...

Psalm 23

(alternating sides) (GNB)

I: The LORD is my shepherd;
   I have everything I need.
He lets me rest in fields of green
      grass
   and leads me to quiet pools of
      fresh water.

II: He gives me new strength.
   He guides me in the right paths,
      as he had promised.

I: Even if I go through the deepest
   darkness,
   I will not be afraid, LORD,
   for you are with me.
   Your shepherd's rod and staff
   protect me.

II: You prepare a banquet for me.
    Where all my enemies can see me;
    you welcome me as an honored
    guest
    and fill my cup to the brim.

I: I know that your goodness and
   love will be with me all my
   life;
   and your house will be my
   home as long as I live.

All: Glory be...

Canticle of Daniel

(alternating sides and response) Daniel 3:52, 58, 62, 64-74, 76, 80-81, 89-90

All: "Blessed are you, O Lord, the God of our fathers,
   praiseworthy and exalted above all forever,
And blessed is your holy and glorious name,
   praiseworthy and exalted above all for all ages.

I: Angels of the Lord, bless the Lord;

Response: praise and exalt him above all forever.

II: Sun and moon, bless the Lord;

Response: praise and exalt him above all forever.

I: Every shower and dew, bless the Lord;

Response: praise and exalt him above all forever.

II: All you winds, bless the Lord;

Response: praise and exalt him above all forever.

I: Fire and heat, bless the Lord;

Response: praise and exalt him above all forever.

II: Cold and chill, bless the Lord;

Response: praise and exalt him above all forever.

I: Dew and rain, bless the Lord;

Response: praise and exalt him above all forever.

II: Frost and chill, bless the Lord;

Response: praise and exalt him above all forever.

I: Ice and snow, bless the Lord,

Response: praise and exalt him above all forever.

II: Nights and days, bless the Lord;

Response: praise and exalt him above all forever.

I: Light and darkness, bless the Lord;

Response: praise and exalt him above all forever.

II: Lightnings and clouds, bless the Lord;

Response: praise and exalt him above all forever.

I: Let the earth bless the Lord;

Response: praise and exalt him above all forever.

II: Everything growing from the earth, bless the Lord;

Response: praise and exalt him above all forever.

I: All you birds of the air, bless the Lord;

Response: praise and exalt him above all forever.

II: All you beasts, wild and tame, bless the Lord;

Response: praise and exalt him above all forever.

All: Give thanks to the Lord, for he is good,
   for his mercy endures forever.
Bless the God of gods, all you who fear the Lord;
praise him and give him thanks,
   because his mercy endures forever."

Leader: The love of God is among us; it calls us to praise and thank him.

(pause)

Word of God   (Philippians 4:5-7) (NAB)

Everyone should see how unselfish you are. The Lord is near. Dismiss all anxiety from your minds. Present your needs to God in every form of prayer and in petitions full of gratitude. Then God's own peace, which is beyond all understanding, will stand guard over your hearts and minds, in Christ Jesus.

This is the Word of the Lord.

All: Thanks be to God.

(pause for silent reflection)

Church Document

Constitution on the Sacred Liturgy #14

Mother Church earnestly desires that all the faithful should be led to that full, conscious, and active participation in liturgical celebrations which is demanded by the very nature of the liturgy. Such participation by the Christian people as "a chosen race, a royal priesthood, a holy nation, a redeemed people" (1 Pet. 2:9; cf. 2:4-5), is their right and duty by reason of their baptism.

In the restoration and promotion of the sacred liturgy, this full and active participation by all the people is the aim to be considered before all else; for it is the primary and indispensable source from which the faithful are to derive the true Christian spirit; and therefore pastors of souls must zealously strive to achieve it, by means of the necessary instruction, in all their pastoral work.

Sharing

(take some quiet moments, then share with one another)

1. What happens when individual/family/parish members do not pray daily?

2. How can we encourage full, active participation of all in the Sacred Liturgy?

3. Does my parish adequately foster the prayer life of its members?

4. What forms can prayer take? Are there prayer forms that have meaning in your life?

Prayer

Leader: Let us ask God to help us persevere in prayer. Anyone who wishes to express aloud special needs may do so....

(pause)

All: God our Father,
you are near to all who open their hearts to your Spirit.
Make us aware of this presence among us.
Give us the desire each day to place our lives before you in
prayer, that we may praise you for your goodness
and be drawn more deeply into your peace.
We ask this through Christ our Lord. Amen.

Blessing

Leader: May the Father of our Lord Jesus Christ enlighten the eyes of our hearts that we might see how great is the hope to which we are called.

Response: Amen.

12. WE ARE CALLED FOR THE VICTORY OF JUSTICE

Jesus does not speak about a change of activities, a change of contacts, or even a change of pace. He speaks about a change of heart. This change of heart makes everything different, even while everything appears to remain the same.

Henri Nouwen

THEME: We Are Called for the Victory of Justice

Prepare: an open Bible, a lighted candle, record, phonograph.

Invitation   **Leader:** (invite all to some quiet moments, then proclaim)
"This is what Yahweh asks of you; only this, to act justly, to love tenderly, and to walk humbly with your God." (from Micah 6:8)

Psalm 72   (alternating sides) paraphrase

I: Teach us to judge with your righteousness, O God;
share with us your own justice,
so we will be able to care for your
people with justice.

II: May the land be fruitful, may
we care for the land which we
do not own but which you, Lord,
have given to us to care for.

I: May we help the needy and the
poor. May we speak out for
their cause before their oppressors.

II: May we worship you, Lord, as
long as the sun shines,
as long as the moon gives its light,
for all ages to come.

I: In our days, may justice and peace grow
in all our land and our hearts.

Let your justice and peace come
down upon us like the rain
on the meadow, the dew on the grass.

II: You, Lord, hear all who
are poor who call upon you,
You have pity on the weak and the poor,
You save those who are needy and neglected.

 I: You, Lord, love the poor,
their lives are precious to you.
You save the lives of those in need.
Lord, you hear the cries of the poor.

II: We pray there may be plenty
of grain in the land;
May the hills and valleys be covered with crops.
Teach us to share your gifts
with one another and all people.

 I: May your name, Lord, be forever blessed!
May your praise and glory be forever!

II: May you be blessed, Lord, Our God,
You, alone, who work wonders for us.
Open our hearts, so that we may be filled with your glory.
You are our God! We praise you!

All: Glory be...

Word of God   (followed by quiet time) paraphrase

Isaiah 58:3-8

Look, you do business on your fast days,
you oppress all your workers;
look, you quarrel and squabble when you fast
and strike the poor person with your fist.

Fasting like yours today
will never make your voice heard on high.
Is that the sort of fast that pleases me,
a truly penitential day for people?

Hanging your head like a reed,
lying down on sackcloth and ashes?
Is that the sort of fast that pleases me,
a day acceptable to Yahweh?

Is not this the sort of fast that pleases me
—it is the Lord Yahweh who speaks—
to break unjust fetters
and undo the thongs of the yoke,

to let the oppressed go free,
and break every yoke,

to share your bread with the hungry,
and shelter the homeless poor,

to clothe the person you see to be naked
and not turn from your own kin?
Then will your light shine like the dawn
and your wound be quickly healed over.

This is the word of the Lord.

All: Thanks be to God.

**Shared
Reflection**

(allow some moments for persons to share)

• What words in the reading spoke to you?

• What does it mean in your life situation to 'share your bread with the hungry,' 'to shelter the homeless poor....'?

• How can you concretely respond to this fast the Lord asks of you?

Litany

Leader: Lord, so many people in our world suffer from injustice, teach us how to reach out to them.

Response: Lord, help us to live justly.

Leader: Lord, we are grateful for our natural resources, air, fuel, food, water and land, help us to use them carefully and to share with others.

Response: Lord, help us to live justly.

Leader: Lord, we are blessed with money, time, talent, help us to extend ourselves to those without the basic necessities of life.

Response: Lord, help us to live justly.

Leader: Lord, strengthen our government leaders and ourselves in our political process to bring about a human world order.

Response: Lord, help us to live justly.

Leader: Lord, you bring peace, show us the way to be peace-makers, help us work for disarmament and for all that will contribute to peace among all people.

Response: Lord, help us to live justly.

Leader: Lord, as we work together to build up this parish community, teach us how to reach out to all, especially the poor and the alienated.

Response: Lord, help us to live justly.

Leader: Let us pray—
The bread which you do not use is the bread of the hungry. The garment hanging in your wardrobe is the garment of the person who is naked. The shoes that you do not wear are the shoes of the one who is barefoot. The money you keep locked away is the money of the poor. The acts of charity you do not perform are so many injustices you commit.

St. Basil the Great

Response: Amen.

Blessing

(turn to the person to your left, place your hand on his/her shoulder and say "The Lord bless you and strengthen you as you work for justice").

Response: Amen.

Closing

Listen to the record, *The Lord Hears the Cry of the Poor* (John Foley, S.J.)

13. THAT ALL MAY HAVE LIFE TO THE FULL
John 10:10

Set your hearts on His kingdom first...and all these other things will be given to you as well. What counts, is where our hearts are. When we worry, we have our hearts in the wrong place. Jesus asks us to move our hearts to the center, where all other things fall into place...to set our hearts on the kingdom, therefore, means to make the life of the Spirit within and among us the center of all we think, say or do.

Henri Nouwen

THEME: That All May Have Life to the Full (Jn. 10:10)

Prepare: lighted candle, open Bible, green plant or other symbol of life.

Invitation

Leader: You must live your whole life according to the Christ whom you have received: Jesus the Lord. You must be rooted in him and built on him and held firm by the faith you have been taught.

Response: Let us join now and praise Him who has given us life. Glory to Christ our Lord. Let us strive to live more fully in Him.

Psalm 33:1-2, 4-5, 18-19

(alternating sides) (NAB)

I: Exult, you just, in the LORD;
   praise from the upright is fitting.
Give thanks to the LORD on the harp;
   with the ten-stringed lyre chant his praises.

II: For, upright is the word of the LORD,
   and all his works are trustworthy.
He loves justice and right;
   of the kindness of the LORD the earth is full.

I: But, see the eyes of the LORD are upon those who fear him,
   upon those who hope for his kindness,
To deliver them from death
   and preserve them in spite of famine.

Glory be...

Word of God   John 14:1-12

'Do not let your hearts be troubled.
Trust in God still, and trust in me.
There are many rooms in my Father's house;
if there were not, I should have told you.
I am going now to prepare a place for you,
and after I have gone and prepared you a place,
I shall return to take you with me;
so that where I am
you may be too.
You know the way to the place where I am going.'

Thomas said, 'Lord, we do not know where you are going, so how can we know the way?' • Jesus said:

'I am the Way, the Truth and the Life.
No one can come to the Father except through me.

If you know me, you know my Father too.
From this moment you know him and have seen him.'

Philip said, 'Lord, let us see the Father and then we shall be satisfied.'
'Have I been with you all this time, Philip,' said Jesus to him 'and you
still do not know me?

'To have seen me is to have seen the Father,
so how can you say, "Let us see the Father?"
Do you not believe
that I am in the Father and the Father is in me?
The words I say to you I do not speak as from myself:
it is the Father, living in me, who is doing this work.
You must believe me when I say
that I am in the Father and the Father is in me;
believe it on the evidence of this work, if for no other reason.
I tell you most solemnly,
whoever believes in me
will perform the same works as I do myself,
he will perform even greater works,
because I am going to the Father.'

Sharing

- What words or phrases spoke to you? Why?

- What does it mean to you that Jesus is your way, your truth, your life?

- Jesus wants us to have life to the full, what does that mean in your life?

Prayer

A Litany to Christ

Leader: I came that they might have life
and have it to the full.   Jn 10:10

All: I am the way, the truth and the life.   Jn 10:6

Leader: I am the bread of life.
I am the bread that came down from heaven.   Jn 6:35, 41

All: Give us this bread always.   Jn 6:34

Leader: I am the gate.
Whoever enters through me will be safe.   Jn 10:9

All: Master...open the door for us.   Mt 25:11

Leader: I am the light of the world.
No follower of mine shall ever walk in darkness.   Jn 8:12

All: Send us your truth and your light.   Ps 43:3

Leader: I am the good shepherd.
The good shepherd lays down his life for the sheep.   Jn 10:11

All: There shall be one flock then, one shepherd.   Jn 10:16

Leader: "I am the resurrection and the life;
whoever believes in me...will come to life."   Jn 11:25, 26

All: For, to me, 'life' means Christ.   Phil 1:21

Leader: I am the searcher of hearts and minds, and
I will give each of you what your conduct deserves.   Rev 2:23

All: Probe me, O God, and know my heart.   Ps 139:23

Leader: I am the Root and Offspring of David,
the Morning Star shining bright.   Rev 22:16

All: Lord, Son of David, have pity on me!   Mt 15:22

Leader: I am the Alpha and the Omega,
the First and the Last, the Beginning and the End!   Rev 22:13

All: Many who are first shall come last and
the last shall come first.   Mt 19:30

Leader: Let us pray together.

Lord Jesus, the Way, the Truth, and the Life,
we pray not to let us stray from you, the Way,
nor to distrust you, the Truth,
no to rest in anyone but you, the Life.
By the Holy Spirit, teach us what to do,
what to believe,
and wherein to take our rest. Amen.   —Erasmus

Blessing   May the Lord give us his help to lead a life worthy of the calling to which he has called; and may we know the fullness of life in the Lord Jesus, with patience, forebearing one another in love, eager to maintain the unity of the Spirit in the bond of peace.

Response: Amen.

14. WHAT YOU HAVE RECEIVED AS GIFT, GIVE AS GIFT

Matthew 10

We pray because the Lord loves us and we wish to respond to His love; then all these other things will be given to us as well.

James V. Gau, SJ

THEME: What You have Received as Gift, Give as Gift (Mt. 10)

Prepare: lighted candle; open Bible; clay pots—some broken, some whole, record and phonograph.

Listen

Record: *Earthen Vessels* (St. Louis Jesuits)

Invitation

Leader: O Lord, let our prayer rise before You like incense,

Response: Fill us with Your love that we may live the whole day in joy and praise.

Prayer

Leader: Let us pray together (slowly, reflectively)

Heavenly Father, we come seeking Your blessing on those who are dear to us, and those whose needs are close to our hearts. You know our longing for them: but You also know, better than we, what is really best for each one of them. Give what You have to give: and if sometimes Your gifts to them seem wrong to us, bless and enlighten us as well.

We pray for all who seek the saving love of a friend and for all who need to know that You are their Friend and Savior.

We pray for those who are trying to give good gifts to those who depend on them: gifts of leadership and advice, gifts of affection and compassion. Deliver them from the temptation to attach strings to their charity, and to try to run the lives of those they would lead and help.

We pray for all communities of faith of our Local Church, especially (here name your parish community). Help them to be faithful in proclaiming the truth about Your love. Deepen our commitment to the one Lord of us all, Jesus Christ, our Savior in time and in eternity. Amen.

Word of God   1 Corinthians 12:4-11 (NAB)

There are different gifts but the same Spirit; there are different ministries but the same Lord; there are different works but the same God who accomplishes all of them in everyone. To each person the manifestation of the Spirit is given for the common good. To one the Spirit gives wisdom in discourse, to another the power to express knowledge. Through the Spirit one receives faith; by the same Spirit another is given the gift of healing, and still another miraculous powers. Prophecy is given to one; to another power to distinguish one spirit from another. One receives the gift of tongues, another that of interpreting the tongues. But it is one and the same Spirit who produces all these gifts distributing them to each as he wills.

Reflection and Sharing   (silence then invite all to share)

1. What gifts do I have to share with my parish community?

2. Were there times when you knew your weaknesses and yet the Spirit helped you reach out to others?

Prayer   **The Litany**

Leader: Lord Jesus, You said, "Blessed are the poor in spirit: the reign of God is theirs." Give us the spirit of poverty and humility.

All: Show to us Your mercy, Lord our God.

Leader: Lord Jesus, You said, "Blessed too are the sorrowing: they shall be consoled." Teach us to share the tears of our brothers and sisters.

All: Show to us Your mercy, Lord our God.

Leader: Lord Jesus, You said, "Blessed are they who hunger and thirst for holiness, they shall have their fill." Give our souls a thirst for justice and love.

All: Show to us Your mercy, Lord our God.

Leader: Lord Jesus, You said, "Blessed are they who show mercy; mercy shall be theirs." Open our hearts with love for our brothers and sisters.

All: Show to us Your mercy, Lord our God.

Leader: Lord Jesus, You said, "Blessed are the single-hearted, for they shall see God." Enlighten our eyes with Your splendor.

All: Show to us Your mercy, Lord our God.

Leader: Lord Jesus, You said, "Blessed too are the peacemakers, they shall be called the children of God." Make us channels of peace and joy.

All: Show to us Your mercy, Lord our God.

Leader: Lord Jesus, You said, "Blessed are those persecuted for holiness' sake, the reign of God is theirs." Make us strong in suffering for the Kingdom.

All: Show to us Your mercy, Lord our God.

Leader: Let us pray with confidence to the Father in the words our Savior gave us:

All: Our Father...

All: For the kingdom and the power and the glory are Yours now and forever. Amen.

Blessing

Leader: May the Lord help us to grow and abound in love for one another.

All: Amen.

Leader: May He confirm our hearts in holiness without blame before God our Father.

All: Amen.

Leader: May He put our faith into action so that we may work for love and preserve hope in Christ Jesus our Lord.

All: Amen.

Closing Hymn   *Grant to Us, O Lord* (Lucien Deiss)

Refrain:

Grant to us, O Lord, a heart renewed, recreate in us your own Spirit, Lord.

15. MARY, MOTHER OF THE CHURCH

"What is the use of praying, if at the very moment of prayer, we have so little confidence in God that we are busy planning our own kind of answer?"

Thomas Merton

THEME: Mary, Mother of the Church

Prepare: open Bible, statue of Mary, lighted candle.

Invitation   (invite to quiet, then pray)

Leader: Praised be God our Father, whose promise of a Redeemer was fulfilled through Mary, as Mother of His Son, Jesus Christ and Mother of all.

Response: Forever and ever. Amen.

Hail Mary   (by sides I and II)

Leader: Hail Mary, of all things in the world most precious

I: Hail Mary, Mother of God, it is thanks to you that the Shepherds chanted with the Angels, "Glory to God in the highest and peace to men of good will."

II: Hail Mary, Mother of God, it is thanks to you that the Wise Men brought their Gifts, guided by the Star.

I: Hail Mary, Mother of God, it is thanks to you that the Apostles were chosen by your Son, the Savior.

II: Hail Mary, Mother of God, it is thanks to you that the Baptist leaped in his mother's womb, and that the torch was lowered before the Light that never can be extinguished.

I: Hail Mary, Mother of God, it is through
you that the ineffable kindness of our God,
of which the Apostle tells, has appeared.

II: Hail Mary, Mother of God, it is from
you that has appeared the true Light,
who says of Himself: "I am the Light of
this World."

I: Hail Mary, Mother of God, it is you who
gave birth to the conqueror of death and hell.

II: Hail Mary, Mother of God, it is you who have
placed in this world its Creator and Redeemer,
our Guide to the Kingdom of heaven.

I: Hail Mary, Mother of God, it is by you that
every faithful heart is saved.

All: We salute you, O treasure worthy of
veneration, that belongs to all. Crown
of virginity! Sceptre of orthodoxy!
Temple that can never be destroyed! Place
of Him who is not held by place! We
salute you, Mary, Mother of God.

(St. Cyril of Alexandria, EN COMIUM)

MAGNIFICAT
Mary's Hymn
of Praise

(Luke 1:46-55) paraphrase

Leader: "My heart praises the Lord; my soul is glad because of God my
Savior

All: because he has remembered me, his lowly servant.

Leader: From now on all people will call me happy,

All: because of the great things the mighty God has done for me.

Leader: His name is holy;

All: He shows mercy to those who fear him, from one generation to another.

Leader: He stretched out his mighty arm

All: and scattered the proud with all their plans.

Leader: He brought down mighty kings from their thrones,

All: and lifted up the lowly.

Leader: He filled the hungry with good things,

All: and sent the rich away with empty hands.

Leader: He kept the promise he made to our ancestors,

All: and came to the help of his servant Israel,

Leader: He remembered to show mercy to Abraham

All: and to all his descendants forever!"

Church Documents

(from the *Constitution on the Church*)

At the message of the Angel, the Virgin Mary received the Word of God

in her heart and in her body, and gave Life to the world. Hence she is acknowledged and honored as being truly the Mother of God and Mother of the Redeemer. Redeemed in an especially sublime manner by reason of the merits of her Son, and united to Him by a close and indissoluble tie, she is endowed with the Supreme office and dignity of being the Mother of the Son of God. As a result she is also the favorite daughter of the Father and the temple of the Holy Spirit. Because of this gift of sublime grace she far surpasses all other creatures, both in heaven and on earth.

At the same time, however, because she belongs to the offspring of Adam she is one with all human beings in their need for salvation. Indeed, she is "Clearly the mother of the members of Christ...since she co-operated out of love so that there might be born in the church the faithful, who are members of Christ their Head." Therefore she is also hailed as a pre-eminent and altogether singular member of the Church, and as the Church's model and excellent exemplar in faith and charity. #53

(allow some time for quiet reflection)

Reading #2   (from the *Apostolic Exhortation, "Marialis Cultis" 1974, Pope Paul VI*)

"...Mary of Nazareth, while completely devoted to the will of God, was far from being a timidly submissive woman or one whose piety was repellent to others; on the contrary, she was a woman who did not hesitate to proclaim that God vindicates the humble and the oppressed, and removes the powerful people of this world from their privileged positions. The modern woman will recognize in Mary, who 'stands out among the poor and humble of the Lord', a woman of strength, who experienced poverty and suffering, flight and exile."

(allow some time for quiet reflection)

Word of God   Luke 11:27-28 (NAB)

While He was saying this a woman from the crowd called out, "Blest is the womb that bore you and the breasts that nursed you!" "Rather," He replied, "blest are they who hear the word of God and keep it."

Reflection   As with Mary, so with us. The word we have heard challenges us to "hear the word of God and keep it." To be proclaimers of the Word, to speak the truth, to seek God's will and to respond to it, is the task of each of us.

Action   (each person is asked to decide on one concrete action to carry out in their life during the next week in response to the word of God)

Prayer   Pray together the Memorare

Remember O most gracious Virgin Mary
that never was it known that anyone who fled to
your protection, implored your help, or sought
your intercession was left unaided.

Inspired with this confidence, we come to you,
O Virgin of virgins, our Mother!
To you we come, before you we stand,
sinful and sorrowful

O Mother of the Word incarnate, despise not our
petitions, but in your mercy, hear and answer us! Amen!

Closing Hymn   *Immaculate Mary* Verse 3

We pray you, O Mother, may God's will be done;

We pray for His glory; may His Kingdom come.

Refrain: Ave, ave, ave, Maria! Ave, ave, Maria!

Outside spiritual reading:

- *The Documents of Vatican II,* "Constitution on the Church in the Modern World." Chapter VIII, The Role of the Blessed Virgin Mary, Mother of God in the Mystery of Christ and the Church.

16. WE ARE CLAIMED FOR CHRIST BY THE SIGN OF THE CROSS

In our prayer, as in our lives, the Lord is leading us in a dance. We miss His rhythm and time, step on His toes and bump into Him, but even these awkwardnesses keep us in relationship with Him. He wants us only to learn to follow His lead.

James V. Gau, SJ

THEME: We Are Claimed for Christ by the Sign of the Cross

Prepare: cross in prominent view; record and phonograph.

Listen

Here I am, Lord (St. Louis Jesuits)

Invitation

Leader: The grace of our Lord Jesus Christ and the love of God and the gift of the Holy Spirit be with you.

Response: And with you.

Prayer

Leader: Lord God, we rely so much on our own power, our own strength. We often look for peace and for hope in our own efforts, in our own words, help us to know fully that it is YOU at work in us. Give us that simple Faith in Jesus' words that He is with us, and through living, dying, rising with Him we will have peace and help and give that to others.

Response: Amen.

Psalm 35

(alternating sides) *Psalms Now* by Brandt

I: It is not easy, Lord, to follow after You.
  While you take the hard road
    with joyous leaps and bounds,
    I stumble over every stone
      and slip into every rut.
  You calmly weather each storm
    and walk fearlessly through the night.
  I am buffeted by the winds,
    and I falter in the darkness.

II: And You always have answers, Lord,
    for those who confront You.
My tongue is thick and clumsy.
I cannot articulate what I feel
    or what they need to hear.
You have the wisdom and the power
    to meet the needs of all about You.
But I am foolish and ineffective,
    and my brothers and sisters turn away from me in disgust.

 I: I have really tried to relate to people about me,
    to reach out in love and concern.
I have shared their sorrows and their joys.
I have shelved my ambitions
    to respond to their needs.
But when I fail to produce what they want,
    or when I am limited in my humanity
        and incapacitated by my personal problems
        and they will have nothing to do with me.
I feel as if I have been used only to be abused.
I am squeezed dry and then cast aside
    as if I were of no further value.

II: Yet I must continue to follow You, O Lord.
It is a hard path to walk,
    and I will falter at times.
I long intensely for an occasional oasis
    along this journey through wind and sand.
I need desperately Your touch of joy and enrichment
    as I labor amidst the blood and tears
        of this distorted world.
I am empty, Lord,
    enable me to sense Your fullness

and grant me the grace and the courage
to be faithful as Your servant.

All: Glory be...

Word of God   Luke 8:4-15

With a large crowd gathering and people from every town finding their
way to him, he used this parable:

'A sower went out to sow his seed. As he sowed, some fell on the edge of
the path and was trampled on; and the birds of the air ate it up. • Some
seed fell on rock, and when it came up it withered away, having no
moisture. • Some seed fell amongst thorns and the thorns grew with it
and choked it. • And some seed fell into rich soil and grew and pro-
duced its crop a hundredfold.' Saying this he cried, 'Listen, anyone who
has ears to hear!'

His disciples asked him what this parable might mean, • and he said,
'The mysteries of the kingdom of God are revealed to you; for the rest
there are only parables, so that

> *they may see but not perceive,*
> *listen but not understand.*

'This, then, is what the parable means: the seed is the word of God.
• Those on the edge of the path are people who have heard it, and then
the devil comes and carries away the word from their hearts in case they
should believe and be saved. • Those on the rock are people who, when
they first hear it, welcome the word with joy. But these have no root;
they believe for a while, and in time of trial they give up. • As for the part
that fell into thorns, this is people who have heard, but as they go on
their way they are choked by the worries and riches and pleasures of life
and do not reach maturity. • As for the part in the rich soil, this is people

with a noble and generous heart who have heard the word and take it to themselves and yield a harvest through their perseverance.'

Reflection

Leader: The Cross is a sign of our faith. The Cross is a reminder of the living, dying, and rising of Jesus. As with the grain of wheat, "unless the grain of wheat falls to the ground and dies, it remains only a grain of wheat"—so with us, Jesus invites us daily into the Paschal Mystery, to live, to die and to rise with Him each day. The cross is a sign of the hope the Lord gave us. The sign of the cross was traced on our forehead at our Baptism and Confirmation. I ask you to come forward now to be signed with the Cross of Jesus Christ. May this signing express your desire to embrace your faith in a new way.

Signing with Cross/Sending

(by leader or pastor)

"_____, I sign you with the Cross of Jesus, you have been claimed as His own."

Response: Amen.

Proclamation

Song, *"Christ has died, etc."*

Prayer

(together)

Father, give us a living Faith; a
Faith by which we will not only accept
Your Word, but act on it every day in
every situation, with every person whom
we touch. Give us faith enough to turn ourselves
completely over to You in complete trust.

You and Your life are most precious gift,
help us to talk about Your work in our lives
to all—We commit ourselves completely to you
now. Here we are Lord, send us. Amen.

Closing Hymn   Join in on: *"Here I am, Lord"*

Here I am, Lord, is it I, Lord? I have
heard you calling in the night. I will go,
Lord, if you lead me. I will hold your
people in my heart.

17. MINISTRY REVIEW:
PARISH COUNCILS,
BOARDS, COMMITTEES

Blessed be God the Father of our Lord Jesus Christ....Before the world was made, he chose us, chose us in Christ, to be holy and spotless, and to live through love in his presence...for his own kind purposes, to make us praise the glory of his grace....He has let us know the mystery of his purpose, the hidden plan he so kindly made in Christ from the beginning to act upon when the times had run their course to the end: that he would bring everything together under

Christ, as head, everything in the heavens and everything on earth. And it is in him that we were claimed as God's own, chosen from the beginning, under the predetermined plan of the one who guides all things as he decides by his own will.

Eph. 1:3-11

THEME: Ministry Review: Parish Councils, Boards, Committees

Introduction

Leader: We are a people called together to serve and to be served. We are accountable to one another and to the parish that calls us. Let us spend some time this evening reflecting on his call and our responsibility as council.

Opening Prayer

Leader: Lord, we come together to acknowledge that we are a people in need of forgiveness. We pray that we may be open to your word and to each other as we look honestly at our lives as Christians and as members of this parish. We ask this in the name of your Son and with the Spirit.

Response: Amen.

Leader: Let us take some moments to reflect on our own roles as we are called to live out our service to this parish.

Catechesis and Evangelization

We are called to be concerned for the continued faith growth of all in our parish family. Let us reflect on this responsibility.

- Do we as a council realize we need to continue our own education and faith growth?

- Do we as a council recognize our responsibility to the total parish community?

- Are we as an education committee selfish in that we do not see ourselves in relation to the total parish?

- Do we as individuals take our membership on this committee seriously?

Social Concerns   We are called to raise the consciousness of our parish on social issues and to act to remedy social ills.

- Do we as a council take the poverty and injustices in our parish and beyond our parish seriously?

- Do we resent having our values challenged by others and by the Gospel message?

- Do we as social concerns committee become so intent upon doing that we often don't spend enough time praying and reflecting on the message?

- Do we as individual members take our responsibility seriously?

Worship and Spiritual Life   We are called to be concerned for the spiritual well-being of the parish. Let us reflect on this responsibility.

- As a Liturgy Committee, do we take seriously our responsibility to call forth active participation of all in the Liturgy?

- Do we as a council recognize the need to deepen our own spiritual growth?

- Do we as a council feel concern for the spiritual well-being of the entire parish?

- Do we as a spiritual life committee get caught up in the idea that we are the most important, rather than seeing ourselves as integral to the parish along with others?

- Do we as individuals, take our membership in this seriously?

Administration   We are called to be concerned for the temporalities of the parish.

- Do we as a council look upon this task as important, but not quite as spiritual as the rest?

- Do we as a council recognize that our budget should reflect our mission and theology as a parish?

- Do we as an administration committee feel we are conscious that our decisions must come from serious reflection on the Mission of the Church of the diocese, our mission as a parish in the light of the Gospel?

- Do we as individual members of the committee take our responsibility seriously?

Parish Life   We are called to integrate the parish activities.

- Do we as a council see the role of parish life as just one of keeping things in order?

- Do we as a council recognize that we can effect a great deal of growth and working together if we integrate what we do?

- Do we become content with just the organization rather than seeing our role in creating an enthusiastic parish community?

- Do we as individual members take seriously our role to build unity and community?

Communications   We are called to disseminate information on parish council activities and other parish activities.

- Do we prepare and publish information about parish council activities?

- Do we assist council committees and other parish organizations in publicizing their activites and promoting their programs?

- Do we make an effort to know the attitudes and concerns of the parish?

- Do we as individual members take seriously this need for accurate communication to members on decisions directly affecting them?

Leader: Let us take some time and silently reflect on how we have carried our mission and where me may have failed.

(you may want to write one thing which you would like to work on to improve)

Read reflectively the reading of the Beatitudes: Matthew 5:1-12.

Seeing the crowds, he went up the hill. There he sat down and was joined by his disciples. • Then he began to speak. This is what he taught them:

'How happy are the poor in spirit,
theirs is the kingdom of heaven.
Happy *the gentle:*
they shall have the earth for their heritage.
Happy those who mourn:
they shall be comforted.
Happy those who hunger and thirst for what is right:
they shall be satisfied.
Happy the merciful:
they shall have mercy shown them.
Happy the pure in heart:
they shall see God.
Happy the peacemakers:
they shall be called sons of God.
Happy those who are persecuted in the cause of right:
theirs is the kingdom of heaven.

'Happy are you when people abuse you and persecute you and speak all kinds of calumny against you on my account. • Rejoice and be glad, for your reward will be great in heaven; this is how they persecuted the prophets before you.'

Time for silence.

Pray Together   We are called to reach out,
        to spread the good news,
        to forgive.
Lord forgive us for the time we have not
        listened and we have not acted in response
        to the Gospel message. Amen.

Blessing   **Leader:** Lord, grant (name of each) the peace that
        only you can give.
Let her/him see her/his role in service
        to you and to the church community in
        our parish.

Then share the peace you have received
with all those present.

Closing Hymn   *Build the City of God* (St. Louis Jesuits)
Play record during peace greeting.

18. RESOURCES FOR
STUDY AND PRAYER

Resources for Study and Prayer

Books

Bausch, William J., with Watkin, Edward. *What's a Parish For?* Chicago: Claretian, 1973.

Bausch, William J. *The Pilgrim Church* (A Popular History of Catholic Christianity) Fides/Claretian.

Clark, Stephen B. *Building Christian Communities: Strategy for Renewing the Church.* Notre Dame: Ave Maria Press, 1972.

Dulles, Avery. *Models of the Church.* New York: Doubleday, 1974.

Fenhagen, James C. *Mutual Ministry.* New York: Seabury Press.

Gremillion, Joseph, ed. *The Gospel of Justice and Peace: Catholic Social Teaching Since Pope John.* Maryknoll, N.Y.: Orbis Books, 1976.

Holland, Joseph. *The American Journey* and *"Social Analysis Linking Faith and Justice,"* New York and Washington, D.C., IDOC and the Center for Concern, 1976.

Keating, Charles J. *The Leadership Book.* New York: Paulist Press.

Keating, Charles J. *Community.* West Mystic, Conn.: Twenty-third Publications, 1977.

Kelly, George A. *The Parish.* New York: St. John's University Press, 1973.

Kennedy, Eugene. *The People Are the Church.* Garden City, NY: Doubleday & Co.

Kilian, Sabbas J., OFM. *Theological Models for the Parish.* New York: Alba, 1977.

Larsen, Earnest. *Spiritual Renewal of the American Parish.* Liguori, MO.: Liguori Publications, 1975.

Larsen, Earnest. *Spiritual Growth: Key to Parish Renewal.* Liguori, MO.: Liguori Publications.

Lyons, Bernard. *Leaders for Parish Councils: A Handbook for Training Techniques.* Techny, Ill.: Divine Word Publications, 1971.

Lyons, Bernard. *Parish Councils: Renewing the Christian Community.* Techny, Ill.: Divine Word Publications, 1967.

Lyons, Bernard. *Programs for Parish Councils: An Action Manual.* Techny, Ill.: Divine Word Publications, 1969.

McBrien, Richard P. *The Remaking of the Church.* New York: Harper & Row, 1973.

O'Neil, David P. *The Sharing Community: Parish Councils and Their Meaning.* Dayton: Pflaum Press, 1968.

Rademacher, William J. *Answers for Parish Councils.* West Mystic, Conn.: Twenty-Third Publications, 1974.

Rademacher, William J. *A Practical Guide for Parish Councils.* West Mystic, Conn.: Twenty-Third Publications, 1979.

Rademacher, William J. *Working With Parish Councils?* Canfield, Ohio: Alba Books, 1977.

Rademacher, William J. *New Life for Parish Councils.* West Mystic, Conn.: Twenty-Third Publications, 1976.

Whitehead, Evelyn, ed. *The Parish in Community and Ministry.* New York: Paulist Press, 1978.

Periodicals

Catholic Trends—Published by U.S. Catholic Conference, 1312 Massachusetts Ave., N.W., Washington, D.C. 20005.

Today's Parish—Published bi-monthly by Twenty-Third Publications, P.O. Box 180, West Mystic, Conn., 06388.

Ministries—Published Monthly by Winston Press, P.O. Box 1076, Skokie, Ill. 60077.

Articles Coleman, William V. "Developing Programs for Parishioner's Needs." *Today's Parish* (May–June, 1977) p. 27.

Coleman, William V. "What is a Parish?" *Today's Parish* (October, 1977) pp. 42-43.

Church Documents *Documents of Vatican II,* Walter W. Abbot, S.J., The America Press, 1966. Especially note:

Declaration on Christian Education

Dogmatic Constitution on the Church

Decree on the Apostolate of the Laity

Pastoral Constitution on the Church in the Modern World

Constitution on the Sacred Liturgy

Other Church Documents *A Call to Action,* (Paul VI, 1971): Apostolic Letter on the Occasion of the Eightieth Anniversary of the Encyclical *Rerum Novarum* of Pope Leo XIII, on May 14, 1971.

Basic Teaching for Catholic Religious Education, prepared by the National Conference of Catholic Bishops in consultation with the Holy See. January, 1973.

General Catechetical Directory, prepared by the Sacred Congregation for the Clergy and approved by Pope Paul VI on March 18, 1971. © Copyright 1971 by the United States Catholic Conference.

Justice in the World, prepared by the Second General Assembly of the Synod of Bishops and confirmed by Pope Paul VI on November 30, 1971.

On Evangelization in the Modern World, an Apostolic Exhortation of Pope Paul VI, December 8, 1975.

Paths of the Church, Encyclical Letter of Pope Paul VI, August 6, 1964.

Peace on Earth (Pacem in Terris), Encyclical Letter of Pope John XXIII, April 11, 1963.

Declaration on Certain Questions Concerning Sexual Ethics, Sacred Congregation for the Doctrine of the Faith, December 29, 1975.

To Teach As Jesus Did, A Pastoral Message on Catholic Education, National Conference of Catholic Bishops, November 1972.

To Live in Christ Jesus, A Pastoral Reflection on Moral Values, National Conference of Catholic Bishops, 1976.

The Parish: A People, A Mission, A Structure, National Council of Catholic Bishops, 1980.

Called and Gifted: The American Catholic Laity, National Council of Catholic Bishops, November, 1980.

Books/ Pamphlets

The New American Bible or the *Jerusalem Bible* are recommended.

Reading Scripture As the Word of God: Practical Approaches and Attitudes by George Martin, Servant Publications, 1975.

The Bible and You (A Scriptographic Booklet) by Channing L. Bete Co., Inc., 1971.

Pathways in Scripture: A Book-by-Book Guide to the Spiritual Riches of the Bible by Damasus Winzen, O.S.B. Word of Life Publications, 1976.

Man Meets God: A Guide to the Great Theme of Revelation in Scripture by Rev. Msgr. David E. Rosage, S.J., published at Immaculate Heart Retreat House, Spokane, Washington, 1973.

Who Do You Say That I Am?: An Adult Inquiry into the First Three Gospels by Rev. Edward J. Ciuba, Alba House, 1974.

Records

By Carey Landry, North American Liturgy Resources, Phoenix, AZ 85029.

1. *I Will Not Forget You*   2. *Glory and Praise*   3. *Abba, Father*
4. *Come Winter, Come Lord*

By St. Louis Jesuits, North American Liturgy Resources, Phoenix, AZ 85029.

5. *Earthen Vessels*   6. *Neither Silver Nor Gold*   7. *Wood Hath Hope*   8. *Lord of Light*

By Gregory Norbet, O.S.B., The Benedictine Foundation, Western Priory Productions, Weston, VT 05161.

9. *Wherever You Go*   10. *Gentle Night*   11. *Listen*   12. *Calm is the Night*